TWENTY
NEW ANTHEMS

FOR SATB

**kevin
mayhew**

We hope you enjoy the music in this book. Further copies
are available from your local Kevin Mayhew stockist.

In case of difficulty, or to request a catalogue,
please contact the publisher direct by writing to:

The Sales Department
KEVIN MAYHEW LTD
Buxhall
Stowmarket
Suffolk IP14 3BW

Phone 01449 737978
Fax 01449 737834
E-mail info@kevinmayhewltd.com

First published in Great Britain in 2003 by Kevin Mayhew Ltd.

© Copyright 2003 Kevin Mayhew Ltd.

ISBN 1 84417 025 X
ISMN M 57024 165 1
Catalogue No: 1450271

0 1 2 3 4 5 6 7 8 9

Cover design by Angela Selfe

Music setter: Donald Thomson
Proof reader: Linda Ottewell

Printed and bound in Great Britain

Contents

Translations of Latin texts

<u>Ave Maria</u> (page 46)

Hail Mary, full of grace, the Lord is with thee, hail Mary:
blessed art thou, blessed art thou among women,
and blessed is the fruit of thy womb, Jesus.
Holy Mary, Mother of God, pray, pray for us sinners,
now and in the hour of our death, pray for us.
Amen.

<u>Tantum Ergo</u> (page 16)

Such a great Sacrament; let us revere with heads bent,
and let the Old Testament give way to the New Observance.
Let faith supply what the senses lack.

To the Father and the Son let there be praise and celebration.
Health, honour and also strength be given, as well as blessing.
To the One who proceeds from them both let equal praise be given.

COME TO ME

Text: Matthew 11:28-29
Music: Elizabeth Hill

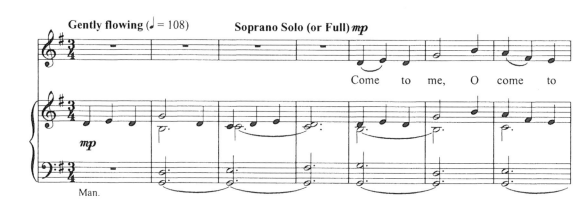

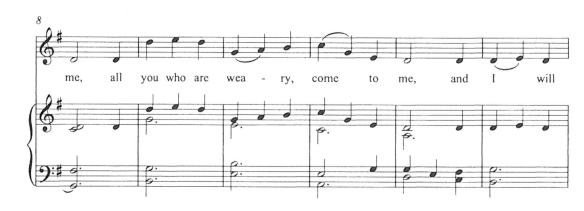

Take my yoke up - on you, and learn from

me, learn from me, and you will find rest un -

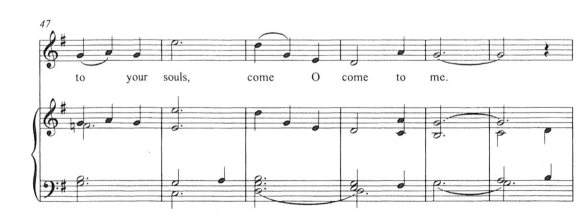

to your souls, come O come to me.

Take my yoke up - on you, and learn from me, learn from me, and you will find rest un - to your souls, come, O come, come to me. Come, O come to me.

For Nick Gale

THIS IS THE MESSAGE

Text: 1 John 3
Music: Alan Rees

O GREAT, ALL-SEEING GOD

Text: Michael Forster
Music: Andrew Fletcher

Our hearts we lift in - deed, and joy - ful praise we sing, to

God who rai - ses up the poor and crowns the shep - herd king!

in per - fect

But great - er mys - t'ry yet in

13

grace de - vised: the Fa - ther's own be - lov - ed Son by

grace de - vised:

Man.

hu - man hand bap - tised!

cresc. poco a poco

Ped.

O grace be - yond com-pare, and

O grace be - yond com - pare, and

Tenors and Basses

TANTUM ERGO

Text: Thomas Aquinas (1227-1274)
Music: June Nixon

See page 5 for translation

to - ri, ge - ni - to - que laus et ju - bi - la - ti -
ju - bi - la -

ju - bi - la - ti -

Man.

o. Sa - lus, hon - or, vir - tus quo - que sit et
- ti - o.

o.

Ped.

be - ne - dic - ti - o. Pro - ce - den - ti ab u -
be - ne - dic - ti - o.

be - ne - dic - ti - o.

Man.

I WILL CALL TO YOU

Text: adapted from Psalm 119:145-147
Music: Simon Lesley

whole heart o - pen, 'Help me, O Lord, as I ob-serve your word.'

Each and ev - 'ry day I'll cry un - to my Lord and Sa - viour,

Man.

'Hear me and help me, my trust is with you, Lord, with you, Lord.'

my trust is with you, Lord, with you, Lord.'

Ped.

COME, GRACIOUS SPIRIT

Text: Simon Browne (1680-1732)
Music: Richard Lloyd

side. The light of truth to us dis-play, and make us know and choose thy way; plant ho-ly fear in ev-'ry heart, that we from God may ne'er de-part.

Lead us to Christ, the liv-ing

(Optional)

(Man.)

heav'n, that we may share full - ness of joy for e - ver there:

lead us to God, our fi - nal rest,

Altos

lead us to God, our fi - nal rest, to be with him for e - ver

Meno mosso

pp

rit

blest, to be with him for e - ver blest.

IN THE SILENCE OF THE STARS

Text: David Adam
Music: Norman Warren

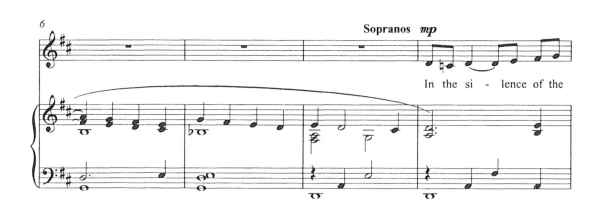

sea, speak, Lord, speak,

Lord.

Tenors and Basses

In the still - ness of this room, in the calm - ing of my mind,

in the long - ing of my heart, speak, Lord,

speak, Lord.

Man.

In the voice of a friend, in the chat - ter of a

(Optional)

child, in the words of a stran - ger, speak, Lord,

speak.

mf unis.

In the op - 'ning of a

mf unis.

Ped.

LET HYMNS OF JOYFUL PRAISE ABOUND

Text: Martin E. Leckebusch
Music: John Jordan

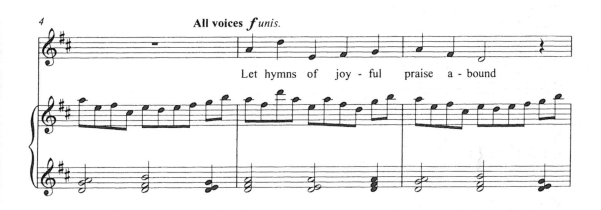

the Lord of end - less ma - jes - ty.

The Lamb who once was cru - ci - fied is seat - ed at his

Fa - ther's side;

his name is hon - oured far and wide –

Descant

our voi - ces join the swell - ing tide.

All voices
f unis.

our voi - ces join the swell - ing tide.

Ped.

Our wor - ship we de - light to bring, for he has gi - ven

Our wor - ship we de - light to bring, for he has gi - ven

IN THE BEGINNING WAS THE WORD OF LIFE

Text: Michael Forster
Music: Betty Roe

fined. In - to cre - a - tion came the Word of life to

those who were his own; scorned and re - ject - ed, still the Word of life made

love e - ter - nal known. Sing al - le - lu - ia with the Word of life,

the Word of truth and grace; whole - ness is of - fered by the

Word of life to all the hu - man race.

Commissioned by the 52nd Sewanee Church Music Conference, Robert Delcamp, Director, 2002

BREAD OF THE WORLD

Text: Reginald Heber (1783-1826)
Music: Malcolm Archer

look on the heart by sor - row bro - ken, look on the tears by sin - ners shed; and be your feast to us a to - ken that by your grace our souls are fed. Bread of the

world in mer - cy bro - ken, wine of the soul in

mer - cy shed, by whom the words of life were

spo - ken, and in whose death our sins are dead:

look on the heart by sor - row

PRAISE THE LORD!

Text: Psalm 113:1-4
Music: Colin Mawby

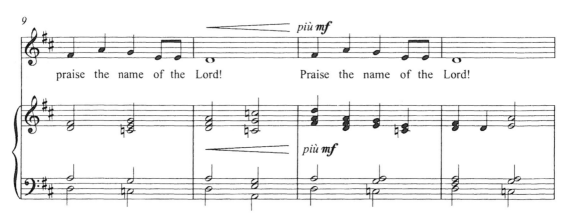

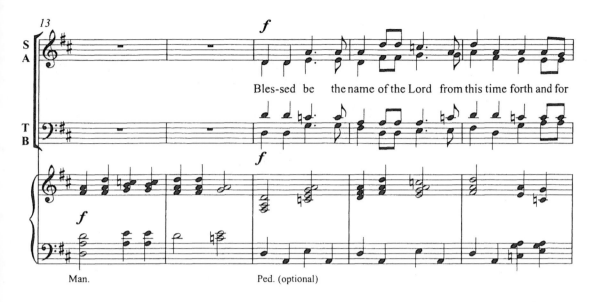

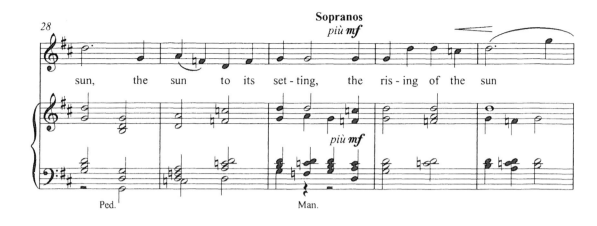

sun, the sun to its set - ting, the ris - ing of the sun

to its set - ting

the name of the Lord is to be praised!

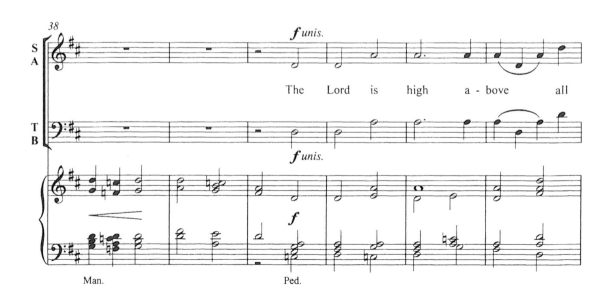

The Lord is high a - bove all

44

na - tions, and his glo - ry a - bove the hea - vens, glo - ry!

For Eric Osborne and the choir of St Andrew's Episcopal Church, Albany, NY

AVE MARIA

Text: Luke 1
Music: June Nixon

See page 5 for translation

© Copyright 2003 Kevin Mayhew Ltd.

for James Devor

CAN IT BE, THAT BREAD AND WINE

Text: Brian Foley (1919-2000), based on John 6
Music: Andrew Wright

(2nd time rit.)

Fine

are more than sign, of Je - sus in me?

Tenors and Basses

mp

Can it be, that bread is flesh, that wine is blood, true food and

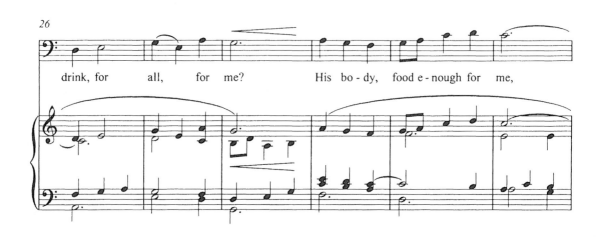

drink, for all, for me? His bo - dy, food e - nough for me,

his blood, true drink e - nough, for all, for me.

mf poco marcato

Je - sus, your word, your thought,

your love in me, are gifts that give your - self to

me. Can it be, that food and drink

poco rit.   D.C. al Fine

make you more pre - sent still to me?

Optional additional verse
mp *espress.*

Oo,   oo,

It must be, Je - sus, that you wish, it must be, to

Oo,   oo,
mp *espress.*

mp *espress.*

give your-self in ev - 'ry way; that you wish to

come your-self, and all your-self, the life of me!

MAY GOD, THE LORD, BLESS US

Text: from the Gelasian and Sarum Rites
Music: John Marsh

bo - dies, save our souls, di - rect our thoughts and

bring us safe to hea - ven, our e - ter - nal home,

where Fa - ther, Son and Ho - ly Spi - rit reign, one

God for e - ver and e - ver. A - men, a -

men, a - men, a - men.

COME, MY WAY, MY TRUTH, MY LIFE

Text: George Herbert (1593-1633)
Music: Michael Higgins

my Light, my Feast, my Strength: such a Light, as shows a feast:

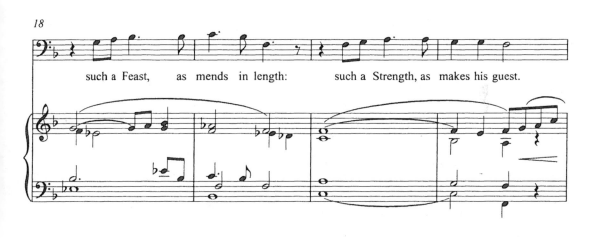

such a Feast, as mends in length: such a Strength, as makes his guest.

Come, my Joy, my

Love, my Heart: such a Joy, as none can move: such a Love, as none can part: such a Heart, as joys in love.

rall.

LORD JESUS, PLANT A SEED OF FAITH

Text: Martin E. Leckebusch
Music: Rosalie Bonighton

Lord Je - sus, plant a seed of faith and let it grow in
Give me a deep - er, rich - er hope, a vis - ion sure and

Last time to Coda ⊕

ser - vant - hood be - comes my ha - bit day by day.
found in no one else Lord, give me more of you!

Last time to Coda ⊕

D.S.

Man. Ped.

⊕ CODA

rall.

(Ped.)

63

GOD OF OUR SALVATION

Text: Martin E. Leckebusch
Music: Robert Jones

God of our sal - va - tion, how you make us
In our ce - le - bra - tions we ex - alt your

strong; how your gifts of joy and com-fort stir our hearts to song!
name, mak - ing known to ev - 'ry peo-ple your un - end - ing fame.

By your lov-ing kind-ness we are freed from fear, draw-ing from your
In your ho-ly pre-sence we re-joice and sing, prais-ing you for

wells of mer-cy wa-ter pure and clear.
all your won-ders, God our migh-ty

King,

God our migh-ty King!

'COME TO ME', SAYS THE LORD

Text: Matthew 11:29-30
Music: Andrew Moore

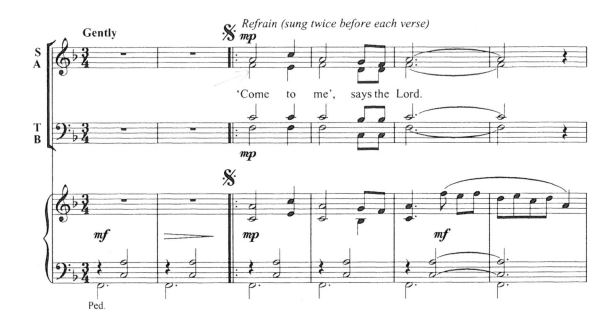

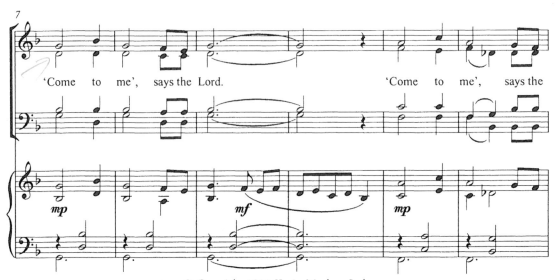

To verses

Lord,　　　　'and　I　will　give　you　rest.'

To verses

Verse 1
mf

1. 'Come,　you who are bur‐dened and　I　will give you rest.　Shoul‐der my yoke　and

mf

mf

rall.　　　　D.S.

learn　from me　for gen ‐ tle　am　I.'

rall.　　　　D.S.

Verse 2

2. 'Shoul - der my yoke and learn from me. Gen - tle am I and

rall. *D.S.*

hum - ble in heart; my bur - den is light.'

Verse 3

3. 'My yoke is ea - sy, my bur - den is light; gen - tle am I and

hum - ble in heart,   you will find rest for your souls.'

Final Refrain

'Come   to   me',   says the Lord.

'Come   to   me',   says the Lord.

'Come to me', says the Lord, says the Lord, 'and

I will give you rest.'

LORD, DISMISS US WITH THY BLESSING

Text: John Fawcett (1740-1817)
Music: Brian Bonsor

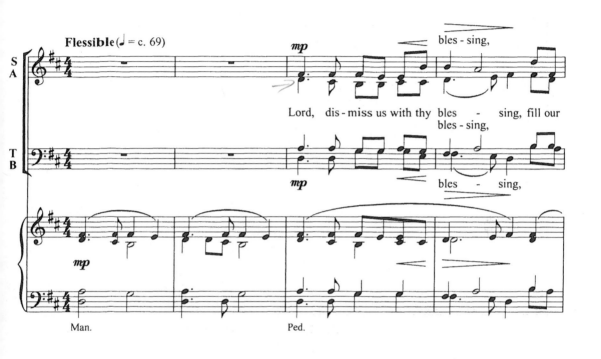

75

MAY THE GRACE OF CHRIST UPHOLD US

Text: Peter Dainty
Music: Martin Setchell

in   peace.   A   -

men.

Solo Oboe 8'